June 19
IREF
5C
6/3/19
use 25

INTIMATE STRANGERS

The Letters of
Margaret Laurence & Gabrielle Roy

INTIMATE STRANGERS

The Letters of
Margaret Laurence & Gabrielle Roy

Edited by Paul G. Socken

University of Manitoba Press

University of Manitoba Press
Winnipeg, Manitoba R3T 2N2
Canada
www.umanitoba.ca/uofmpress

Cover and text design: Terry Gallagher, Doowah Design Inc.

Library and Archives Canada Cataloguing in Publication
Laurence, Margaret, 1926-1987.

Intimate strangers : the letters of Margaret Laurence &
Gabrielle Roy / edited by Paul Socken.

Includes bibliographical references.

ISBN 0-88755-177-7

1. Laurence, Margaret, 1926-1987--Correspondence.
2. Roy, Gabrielle, 1909-1983--Correspondence. 3. Novelists,
Canadian (English)--20th century--Correspondence.
4. Novelists, Canadian (French)--20th century--Correspondence.
I. Roy, Gabrielle, 1909-1983. II. Socken, Paul, 1945- III. Title.

PS8523.A86Z496 2004   C813'.54   C2004-906494-0

The University of Manitoba Press gratefully acknowledges the financial
support for its publication program provided by the Government of Canada
through the Book Publishing Industry Development Program; the Canada
Council for the Arts; the Manitoba Arts Council; and the Manitoba
Department of Culture, Heritage and Tourism.

Printed in Canada

In Memory of Pierre H. Dubé

"A friend may well be reckoned the masterpiece of Nature"

— RALPH WALDO EMERSON

❈ TABLE OF CONTENTS ❈

ACKNOWLEDGEMENTS

I undertook the publication of the letters of Gabrielle Roy and Margaret Laurence after working in the field of French-Canadian and Québécois literature for over thirty years. However, my experience with English-Canadian literature, and Margaret Laurence in particular, is very limited. I am deeply grateful for the extraordinary kindness shown to me by eminent Laurence specialists who shared their knowledge with me and offered very helpful advice and encouragement: Clara Thomas, John Lennox and Susan Warwick of York University, Donez Xiques of Brooklyn College, and Lyall Powers of the University of Michigan, Ann Arbor. Their assistance was indispensable.

The staff at the York University Archives and Special Collections was very accommodating and helpful. I would like to acknowledge their assistance.

I want to thank the Fonds Gabrielle Roy and the estate of Margaret Laurence for permission to publish these letters.

In February 1976, when Margaret Laurence first wrote to Gabrielle Roy, she said of Roy's *The Road Past Altamont* that "I shared something of that Manitoba background and could understand and feel it so well." It was the beginning of a seven-year correspondence. The two writers shared their mutual admiration for each other's work, but, more than that, discovered the elements and issues they held in common as Canadian, prairie, women writers who cared passionately about their work and political and cultural world. These letters express hope, frustration, caring, daily trivia, joy, and fear. They are a remarkable glimpse into the private lives of two of Canada's greatest writers who had experienced great success in their work and were now struggling with their capacity to continue.

Both writers were born in small-town Manitoba, Roy in 1909 in St. Boniface, and Laurence in 1926 in Neepawa. Both had left Canada before they began to commit to their writing, and both remained forever imprinted with their prairie roots. When Laurence and Roy began this correspondence in early 1976, they were also at important stages in their lives. In 1974, Laurence had completed her

Manawaka series with the publication of her final novel, *The Diviners*. It met with great critical and popular success, and won Laurence her second Governor-General's Award for fiction. *The Diviners* was her last published work of fiction for adults. The remaining years of her life were devoted to writing smaller pieces — such as several books for children — and to social activism. After many years of living in England, Laurence had returned to Canada in 1970, and settled in the village of Lakefield, Ontario, outside Peterborough. During this period she became the chancellor of Trent University and the first president of the Writers' Union of Canada. By the mid-1970s, Margaret Laurence was very much a public figure, one engaged in many of the political and social debates of the time.

Gabrielle Roy's first novel, *Bonheur d'occasion (The Tin Flute),* had been an immediate sensation when it was published in 1945. Despite the great success of her work throughout the following two decades, by the 1960s it seemed that Roy's reputation had begun to be eclipsed by a wave of new writers and styles. During this period she dedicated herself to her autobiography, which was published posthumously in 1984. Nevertheless, in spite of many obstacles, in the last period of her life she wrote what many would consider Roy's most beautiful and mature works: *Un Jardin au bout du monde* (1975), *Ces Enfants de ma vie* (1977), *Fragiles Lumières de la terre* (1978), and the posthumous *La Détresse et l'enchantement*. She won the Governor-General's award for *Ces Enfants de ma vie* in 1978, among a host of other prizes and awards, and by the late 1970s her work enjoyed a real revival.

At the time of this correspondence, Roy was beset by health and personal problems. She had been ill for many years and now complained about her weakness to friends and in her correspondence. She suffered from arthritis, asthma, and heart problems to such an extent that her later years were taken up, to a large measure, by coping with her increasing distress. She was also troubled by family burdens. Her beloved sister, Bernadette, had died in 1970. Without Bernadette, Roy became largely responsible for overseeing the care of their sister Clémence, who had been emotionally unwell since childhood. In 1979, another sister, Adèle, published a scandalously vindictive autobiography that portrayed Roy as mean-spirited and self-centred. Although few found Adèle's portrait credible, her book was one of many worries that contributed to the weakening of Roy's health. By the time of her last letter to Laurence in March 1980, Roy wrote she was "fighting my way through with poor hands, poor breath, poor heart." Eventually, these burdens were too much for her, and Roy died of a heart attack in July 1983.

Margaret Laurence, although 17 years younger than her counterpart, was soon also dealing with ill health. By the early 1980s, she had begun to suffer from arthritis and eye problems, and in 1986 was diagnosed with lung cancer. After it became clear that her cancer was inoperable, Laurence took her own life in January 1987.

Gabrielle Roy never enjoyed attending social or public functions, small or large, claiming it took time from her work. It may have been her work, her ill health, her shy nature, or a combination of all these factors that made her withdraw and assiduously guard her privacy. What is clear is that Laurence's more outgoing, exuberant nature and more robust exchange with life were qualities that the older, frailer Roy truly admired

A mutual friend, Joyce Marshall, helped to initiate this relationship between Margaret Laurence and Gabrielle Roy. Marshall, a novelist, broadcaster, and translator, had met Roy in 1959 and translated three of her books, including *Enchanted Summer*, for which she won a Governor-General's Award for Translation in 1976. Beginning in the 1960s,

Marshall had helped to introduce Roy to the work of many of her English-Canadian contemporaries, especially Laurence. Laurence and Marshall had become friends through their work together in the newly formed Writers Union of Canada.

Laurence and Roy met in person only once, at a conference on Canadian literature in Calgary in 1978. These letters indicate they also spoke on the phone, and were avid readers of each other's work. All their letters to each other are written in English. This troubled both writers, but for different reasons. Roy often apologized for what she felt was her inferior English. In fact, her English was very good indeed, although sometimes flawed, and her letters are presented exactly as she wrote them. Margaret Laurence, on the other hand, was intensely conscious of her inability to correspond with Roy in French, and was highly apologetic for this. As a Canadian, she felt it was her duty to know French, and she took great pride in her daughter's fluency in Canada's other official language.

There are just thirty-two letters in this correspondence. Even in so few letters, they cover many topics, ranging from the humorous – Laurence's recounting the tale of a parade in "Lakefield, Literary Capital of the World" – to the gravely serious – the Quebec election of

1976, which disturbed both women ("How are we to write about our country at this hour," Roy asks in one letter, "if not with our sorrowful hearts, our pain and regrets"). They also discussed the censorship and banning of *The Diviners* and the struggle to cope with debilitating illness at the same time as trying to write.

As might be expected, most of the correspondence focusses on their writing. Each profoundly admires the work of the other. In one letter, Laurence tells Roy, "There is something so crystal-clear and flowing and pure about your writing.... And it is the quality of gentleness and tenderness in it, combined with the knowledge of life's pain and sadness, that speak to me." In turn, Roy wrote, "As always with your books, I right away felt immersed in a strong sure element, and let myself by borne away with an acquiescence which comes only, I suppose, with perfect trust." Yet, other topics are the subject of several letters: Roy's flying ants, Laurence's fiftieth birthday party, the beauty of a river at evening.

In an article on the Margaret Laurence-Gabrielle Roy letters, Martine Fisher* notes that the correspondence,

---

* "C'est une étrange profession que nous avons choisie, Gabrielle, ou plutôt qui nous a choisies": la correspondance avec Margaret Laurence in Gabrielle Roy inédite, sous la direction de François Ricard et Jane Everett, Éditions Nota Bene, 2002.

which lasted from February 1976 to January 1983 (Roy died later that year), consists of one letter every two months during the first year, then one every four months, and then a silence of two years after September 1980, broken by Laurence. Fisher gives a good overview in French of some of the themes and preoccupations of the two writers. She suggests there be studies of their commentaries on their own and each other's writing, their style, the political situation in Quebec, and their common Manitoba heritage. She quotes Susan Ward on the emergence of a new literary myth – the figure of the artist as heroine – and concludes that this myth applies to Gabrielle Roy and Margaret Laurence as they attempt to achieve a balance between the demands of their craft and their life.

Reading these letters, one can understand why Laurence and Roy reached out to one another in these final years. Notwithstanding their obvious differences, they were kindred spirits. Both in failing health, beset by loss and problems, concerned about their legacy, and worried about the fate of their country and social justice, theirs were two worlds that touched. Both did have other, closer, friends, but this special, late-flowering friendship was meaningful because it was so firmly based on shared values and a shared heritage.

A note on the letters

The original letters by Margaret Laurence found
in this volume are stored in the Fonds Gabrielle Roy (MSS
1982-11/1986-11) in the National Library in Ottawa.
The original letters by Gabrielle Roy found in this volume
are stored in the "Margaret Laurence Papers" in the York
University Archives and Special Collections, Toronto
(1980-001/004 and 1982-002/004). York University
possesses photocopies of the Margaret Laurence letters as
well. Laurence's letters are mostly typewritten, while Roy's are
handwritten.

There are thirty-two letters in total, eighteen
from Margaret Laurence and fourteen from Gabrielle Roy.
Fifteen of the Laurence letters to Roy have been published
in J.A. Wainwright's *A Very Large Soul.** Four Roy letters to
Laurence have been published in a special issue of *Canadian
Woman Studies/Les Cahiers de la femme.***

---

* J.A. Wainwright, *A Very Large Soul: Selected Letters from Margaret Laurence to
Canadian Writers* (Dunvegan: Cormorant Books, 1995).
** "Letters from Gabrielle Roy to Margaret Laurence," *Canadian Woman Studies/Les
Cahiers de la femme* 18, 3 (1987): 52-53. They are the letters dated March 27,
1976; March 31, 1976; November 15, 1976; and June 4, 1977.

INTIMATE STRANGERS

The Letters of
Margaret Laurence & Gabrielle Roy

8 Regent St., Box 609, Lakefield, Ontario, K0L 2H0

15 Feb. 76

Dear Gabrielle Roy –

Joyce Marshall* gave me your address, so I'm venturing to write to you. Joyce said you had mentioned that you'd like to meet me, and I was so very pleased to hear it – it's a cliché, I know, but I have admired your work for a long time. You know how there are sometimes scenes from novels which continue to inhabit the mind forever after? For me, one such scene is the one in The Tin Flute in which Rose-Anna is told that Daniel has leukemia, and not told that it will be fatal. There are many other scenes (and characters) in your work which remain with me always, but somehow that is one scene which has in a sense grown in power in my mind throughout the years – when I first read it, I was in my early twenties, and did not yet have my children; later, when my daughter was a month old, in England, she developed a mysterious illness with convulsions . . it turned out that she had had her yellow fever and smallpox injections too close together and in the wrong order (we were going out to West Africa), a fact which

* Author and translator Joyce Marshall translated Gabrielle Roy's *The Road Past Altamont, Windflower,* and *Enchanted Summer.*

medical science only discovered several years later. At the time, they didn't know what was wrong with her, so they told me she probably had spiral meningitis – it was, in a sense, the reverse of Rose-Anna's experience, for they neglected to tell me that the disease was not always fatal. In my terrible pain, believing she would die, I remembered Rose-Anna. Although the circumstances of my life and Rose-Anna's could hardly be more different, I have always felt I knew that woman awfully well. There is a part of her in me, the part that never ceases to be concerned over one's children, even though mine are now 20 and 23.

I have recently received from Joyce the NCL edition of THE ROAD PAST ALTAMONT.* I had read it when it first came out, and loved it, and felt I shared something of that Manitoba background and could understand and feel it so well. I think Joyce's Introduction is splendid – probably unique, in a way; I don't remember ever having read such an essay before, in which the translator can speak from a unusually close position to the work and can therefore talk of it with a special kind of knowledge.

Since I finished THE DIVINERS, several years ago, I have virtually written nothing except some articles and a

---

* Margaret Laurence usually used capitals in typing the titles of books.

---

lot of book reviews. No real writing. I'd like to try to write a children's book. I'm a bit hesitant about beginning, but no doubt will do so. I am assured by Sheila Egoff, in her book about Canadian children's literature, THE REPUBLIC OF CHILDHOOD (Republic? Why not Dominion??) that animal fantasies are looked upon with scorn by the young of today. I suspect that she herself doesn't much like them – I'm not sure about children. Anyway, mine will be an animal fantasy because that is what I want to write. I have done one children's book – an animal fantasy, JASON'S QUEST, which Ms. Egoff calls "the most disappointing book in all of Canadian children's fiction". If one is going to fail, by all means let us do so grandly! However, one cannot in the end be guided by critics or even potential readers.

        If ever you have time, I would so much like to hear from you. Don't, however, feel any obligation. I really just wanted to write and send you my greetings and my thanks for your work.

Sincerely,

[signed Margaret Laurence] Margaret Laurence

Dear Gabrielle —

Thanks so very much for your letter,* which
delighted me. It is strange that we should hesitate to approach
other writers — I had the same sense of diffidence before
I wrote to you. But we are, after all, members of the same
tribe, all of us. There is this growing sense of true community
among the Anglophone writers in Canada, over the past
couple of years, owing mainly, I believe to the Writers' Union.
I don't doubt that the same is true among Francophone
writers. If only we could get together more, across the
language barrier.

Speaking of languages, two of my novels, THE STONE
ANGEL and THE DIVINERS are going to be translated into
French, by the publishing firm Le Cercle du Livre de France,
in Montreal. THE STONE ANGEL is being translated by Claire
Martin, which pleases me very much, needless to say. The only
other of my novels to be translated into French as yet is THE
FIRE-DWELLERS, which was done by a publisher in France. At

---

* There is no record of the letter Gabrielle Roy sent to Margaret Laurence in
response to the first letter dated 15 February 1976.

the time when they had just taken the book, Naim Kattan was in Paris, and tried to persuade them to get a French-Canadian translator, but they wouldn't. Alas. So I am very pleased that these other 2 books are being done by a French-Canadian firm.

I'm glad to hear that you want to write a children's book. There is such a desperate need in this country for good children's books – not that that is any reason for writing one! I haven't yet begun mine – I sense that it is not quite ready to be written, as yet, but I hope it will be soon. I've just completed work on a collection of essays and articles, written over the years, and I think McClelland & Stewart will publish it in the fall. A good many of them are travel articles. Not deathless prose, but fairly interesting, I hope. Jack McClelland and I are having our usual amiable battle over the title . . . he doesn't like my title, and I refuse to allow him to choose one, naturally. I have called it after one of the articles . . "Where the World Began", which refers to my world beginning in a small prairie town.

THE DIVINERS is coming under fire in my own community here, I am sorry to say. It was on the Grade 13 high school course, and a parent complained that it was "obscene" because it contains some so-called four-letter words and a few sex scenes – the first are essential to the narrative line and the revelation of character. A local school trustee, who is a fundamentalist, has got into the act and stated in the Peterborough Examiner that only "true" Christians have the right to choose material for English courses (this would, I suspect, exclude not only those of the Jewish faith, but also Roman Catholics, Anglicans, etc etc!). He admits he reads only the Bible (I can't quarrel with his reading of that – it is a book I frequently read myself) and "religious writings". He has not read THE DIVINERS, because "one does not have to wade in the muck to know what it is all about". I realize that people like this will always, alas, be with us, but I cannot help feeling hurt at having my work so vastly misunderstood. There have been some very heartening and supportive letters in the papers, and also some very nasty ones. The nasty ones all state that the people who are writing them have not read my novel, but they somehow "know" it is corrupting the young! It will be taken to a Textbook Review Committee, so we shall see. But the fundamentalist trustee is lobbying against it as hard as he can. In fact, at its deepest level, it is a novel about God's grace. But even if trustee Telford read it, I doubt that he would see that. Well, we must survive such unpleasant episodes.

I'm sending you a copy of the novel, together with a little record of the songs. The music was composed by a friend, Ian Cameron.

I hope your health is improving, and that you will be able to get outdoors when the spring arrives. And thanks so much again for your letter.

With all best wishes,

[signed] Margaret

Dear Margaret

     I received your letter and book yesterday. I was made very happy by the gift of the book, but remain confused. The moment my letter to you had left, confessing that I had not as yet read The Diviners, I felt that I had been maladroit, that a woman as generous as you would seize on the occasion to offer it to me. I cannot help feeling happy just the same over the book and its precious inscription.

     I read the first chapter last night in bed before sleep. As always with your books, I right away felt immersed in a strong, sure element, and let myself be borne away with an acquiescence which comes only, I suppose, with perfect trust. How is it that starting on one of your books, one knows instantly that one is not to be imposed upon or let down? I shall write soon to tell you more of my pleasure in reading you. Also to answer some of your questions.

     I wouldn't let the attack from the school board worry me too much if I were you. After all, it places you in the company of Flaubert, Lawrence and several others among the greatest. It is true that the attack in their case did not come from school boards. Perhaps – and I dwell on <u>perhaps</u>, having not read yet – we offer books of too vast an experience to young people as yet too young. I know that I always feel a little embarrassed when I hear of adolescents of fifteen or sixteen reading and studying The Tin Flute at school. I don't think we had them in mind – do you? – when we wrote our books. But there are no reasons for attacking you so vilely. To speak of your books as "muck" shows where the muck is: in the mind of the vilefinder.* I can understand how painful it must be to you to be attacked, as it were, by your neighbors.

The good news in your letter is that Claire Martin will translate The Stone Angel. She has a wonderful style of her own, incisive, terse, brilliant – not at all yours which is far more resonant of sorrow and compassion – but she must be quite able – artist as she is – to bend her talent to fully capture your own.

By all means stick to Where the World Began** which to me sounds right, looks good, and, furthermore, is "inviting."

You are so good as to inquire about my health. Well, for months the cold was my worst enemy. Now the thaw is. In

---

* Gabrielle Roy means "vilifier".
** The title of one of the chapters in *Heart of a Stranger,* 1976.

a little while the new foliage will be my undoing. The solution might be to live atop a column in the midst of the desert such as Simon the Stylite.* But no, I love my friends too much to perch myself beyond their reach. As a matter of fact, I am quite well sometimes in the summer when at Petite-Rivière-St. François, my country retreat, I am visited by those lovely south-west winds blowing across most of the continent straight from our native prairie. Their amiable softness neither too damp nor too dry, do me so much good that I think myself cured for ever – during twenty-four hours. Or is it their flow of remembrances which bring back for an instant the well-being of youth?

Dear Margaret, please do not feel too unhappy over the misunderstanding about The Diviners. Instead try to think of the so numerous creatures to whom you have given the incredible joy of feeling, at last, understood and seen soul to soul.

Yours
Gabrielle

---

* St. Simeon Stylites (387–459), a Christian ascetic, was revered as a miracle worker. He established himself on top of a pillar twenty-one metres high, near Antioch, where he spent the rest of his life preaching to the people.

Dear Margaret,

I have not been able to lay down The Diviners till I
had finished reading the book. Then I agreed completely with
you. It is — and not only at its deepest level but quite clearly
so — a book about the grace of God. The wonderfully apt
title applies fully in every sense. It is a search for water, truth,
identity, words, but, beyond all that, for whoever or whatever
compels us to the endless search. It is a strong and beautiful
book. Your characters are stronger, if possible, than any you
have created so far. Christie, Prin, Morag of course, Jules,
Pique, all stand out memorably, even lesser people such as
McRaith and the unfortunate Bridie, or Brooke, but are there
secondary characters in this book? Only, I suppose, in the
sense that some take less place. Otherwise they are all fully
present, even the long gone Catherine Parr Traill whose voice
rises so naturally in the wilds of weeds and times. I wouldn't
be surprised if I remembered them all quite distinctly in six
months, in a year, the test that establishes in the end that a
book will last.

---

* There is no record of Margaret's response to the previous letter.

As for the misunderstanding that flared up about it, I can't say that it really surprises me. How many readers are there, here or elsewhere, to see that sex scenes are not put in a book just for the lure but to point at the ambiguity and sadness and greatness of the human condition, not many as yet, you must agree. And the kind that you describe in your letter are certainly not that type of reader, through no fault of theirs in a sense, therein lies the misery of it all. It is a very mature book and few people are, one must face the truth.

One thing troubled me some as I read, it is your apparent rejection of pathetic fallacy. I who use it as I breathe! Well maybe it is right for you to shun it and right for me to give in to it. I still think of <u>I wandered as lonely as a cloud</u>* as a much truer echo of the plaintive human heart than most lines from Browning, however strong he is.

Yet, without pathetic fallacy, you achieve a perfect accord with nature. I shall not soon forget your description of swallows — perhaps because I myself have watched them endlessly, but your observations, I see, are more accurate than mine. Which makes me a little envious.

---

* Roy misquotes here. The actual quote is "I wandered lonely as a cloud" (Wordsworth).

I hope things will straighten up with the school trustee.

Thanks again so very much for the gift of the book.

With affectionate wishes
Gabrielle

Dear Gabrielle:

Please forgive me for not having replied sooner to your two good letters. I shall tell you presently of some of my activities these past two hectic months. But first, thank you for your response to THE DIVINERS. It means more to me (your comments, I mean) than I can possibly say. As for the pathetic fallacy – I've often used it myself. It was just one of those things that Morag learned about at that age, and probably used the form herself later on! I myself tend to think very anthropomorphically, and attribute feelings of deep parental concern to the swallows, which they may not have, or not in the same way as I imagine. Yes, they do, though!

During April and May, it seems I had about six deadlines for book reviews, one of them a fascinating and definitive history of the Japanese in Canada, but a book of some 445 pages of fine print, and although I am normally a pretty fast reader, this one took days to read. I also went out to a number of Canadian literature classes at Trent university and various high schools where they were studying one of my books. I worked for a solid week, together with several others, on the final draft of the Writers' Union standard contract, which our members can use as guidance when signing a contract with a publisher. I attended the Writers' Union conference (3 days) in Ottawa. I also, in between all this, had to try to keep up with the flow of business correspondence, plus doing final revisions on a manuscript of my own . . a book of essays, to be called HEART OF A STRANGER (the title is from Exodus) which will be published in the autumn. Then, the middle of May I went out to High Prairie, Alberta, 225 miles north of Edmonton, to visit with my brother and his wife and their two daughters, for a week. What beautiful country it is! Great stretches of farmlands, with those vast prairie fields all set out in sections and quarter sections, and the soil that true black colour that always has seemed the only proper colour for soil to be. In between are forests of poplar, spruce, pine. It is much more northerly than my own (and your) part of the prairies, but it still felt like home. I think you are right – I am basically a prairie writer, even though I have written of other places. My emotional attachment to the prairies remains very strong.

So I have been having a busy time, but it's all been interesting and worthwhile. I'm now out at my summer cottage, which is about 20 miles from Lakefield, on the same

river, the Otonabee. The river is the same as I described it in
THE DIVINERS — I wrote most of the novel here and the river
just seemed naturally to flow through the book. I hope to have
a reasonably restful and quiet summer here. It's lovely to come
back in the spring and find everything the same. The only
difference this year is that a family of upstart sparrows has
taken over the swallow abode outside my front window! I hate
to sound snobbish, but they are turning it into a slum — bits
of dried grass straggling all over the place! However, perhaps it
will be interesting to compare their young ones' development
with that of the swallows' young. The only snag at the moment
here is the huge numbers of mosquitoes. Today is cloudy, so
they are out in their droves. Luckily, the whole front of my
cabin is a huge glass window, so even when I'm inside I feel
almost as though I were outside.

I wonder how things are with you, and hope
everything is going well.

With very best wishes,
[signed] Margaret

Dear Margaret,

Thank you so much for your very good letter so full of interesting news. I envy you your superb energy. I could not accomplish a quarter of what you achieve. Until I have time for a longer letter, accept my warm regards, and my children's story* going to you under separate cover.

Gabrielle

---

* *Ma Vache Bossie* (Montréal : Leméac, 1976), 45 pp.

Dear Gabrielle:

Please forgive my long delay in replying to your letter and in thanking you for the children's book. I loved the book — my son's girl friend translated it for me, very humbly, saying she could only give an approximation of your style and felt totally inadequate, etc, but it did give me the gist of the story. It's a very touching story and I'm sure that many many children will take it to their hearts. You were very fortunate in the illustrator — the pictures are beautiful.[*]

I am only just now getting into my stride again, after slipping on the dock at my cottage, towards the end of June, and breaking a rib. A very stupid thing to do — these things happen so fast that one can scarcely believe for a few moments that they've happened at all. Complications developed in the form of pleurisy, and I had a bad couple of weeks. I'm fine now, but not very energetic. However, I've been doing a great deal of reading, which is really what I wanted most to do this summer.

---

[*] Louise Pomminville illustrated *Ma Vache Bossie (My Cow Bossie)*.

I've been out at my cottage on the river since early June, and I go home once a week to do shopping and laundry and collect the mail. It is simply lovely here – the river changes constantly with the times of day, and I never get tired of watching it. A few weeks ago my two children (son 21 this month, daughter 24 also this month) put on a splendid birthday party out here for my 50th birthday. They invited about 30 friends, mostly from Toronto, and prepared a marvellous meal. It was a very memorable day, and I was so touched that they would want to do that for me. It was an odd day in some ways, because it nearly turned into a tragedy. A large number of people were visiting the old Yugoslavian man who is my neighbor on one side, and were celebrating the 21st birthday of one young man of their party. The young man went in swimming too soon after a large meal, and got cramps. It took us a moment to realize that he was in trouble, and as he was in the river beside our place, the people next door didn't even realize his plight. There was a second of dreadful recognition, when all of us who were outside my cottage realized that none of us was a powerful enough swimmer to go to his aid. One of my other neighbors, a close friend and a writer,[*] flashed into our row boat and started out.

[*] Perhaps Don Bailey.

I ran into my cottage to find the one person who might be able to help – a young friend named Peter whom we've known for a long time (he was one of the young Elm Cottage Canadians who stayed with us in England). I told him the young man was drowning, and Peter, who is extremely thin and frail looking but is in fact an excellent swimmer, simply flew out of the house and dived in. He managed to get an arm around the young man and raise him out of the water sufficiently until Don got there with the rowboat. Another minute and the kid would have drowned. It was really like a miracle.

I am trying to discover the name of more wildflowers this summer. I have a lot of wildflower and weed books, and I try to identify a few more each day. I have even found locally some of the species whose delightful names I listed in THE DIVINERS, names such as Rough Daisy Fleabane, which to me suggests a dance hall girl of the Klondike era!

I hope the summer is being kind to you.

All best wishes,
[signed] Margaret

ps. I'm sending this to your home address as I'm not sure you will still be in Petite-Riviere-St. Francois.

Dear Margaret,

I am quite ashamed not to have yet answered your two lovely letters which I so enjoyed. The first one, written last spring, I believe, or in early summer, charmed me especially with its lovely description of your visit to, is it to High or Grand Prairie; and of the black loam there stretching to reach the perfectly blue sky. So many times, when I traveled in those parts, as a young journalist, I was struck by the beauty of this exposed loam and I agree with you; this is the real Prairie; it even is, to me, the heart of Canada, although I don't know how to explain my feeling. Something rich, mysterious, solid and yet so heavenly!

Your second letter also appealed to me, this time I think because of all those homey, lovely details about your daily life at the cottage, your birthday celebrated there by your children — how lovely of them, and how young you are still — with all those remarkable books behind you — ; also because of your link with the river which you make me feel very strongly, in your book as well as in your letter.

So I am sending my humble <u>Enchanted Summer</u>, where "<u>my</u>" great river also plays an important role perhaps the first one, in the hope that it will bring you an hour or so of gladness and freshness.

Good luck, my dear, in your work and in your daily life full of generosity to others.

Affectionately yours
Gabrielle

Dear Gabrielle:

I must apologize for having been so long in writing
to thank you for ENCHANTED SUMMER. Naturally, I wanted to
read it before replying, and seemed to have a lot of book-
review deadlines and so on, just at that time.

I can't tell you how truly enchanting I found the
book! The river – "your" river – is so much more vast than
the little Otonabee where I have my cottage, but nonetheless,
so very much in the book reminded me of my own summers,
and so many aspects of the book really spoke to me. I love
Monsieur Toong – I, too, love to listen to the bullfrogs in the
river in the spring of the year. Our bullfrogs here are, I think,
Anglophone, as contrasted to your Francophone ones! Ours
say "Gronk!" Scarcely as mellifluous as the Francophone
"Toong", but perhaps with a certain dramatic emphasis.
I loved very much, too, your description of the kildeer . .
anxious parents that they are. So many times when I've been
out walking near my cottage, I've met with the same nervous
birds, hysterically trying to lead me away from their nest. How
accurately you describe it, and how poetically at the same

time! As for the possible charges of being "anthropomorphic" in our attitudes to birds and animals – in THE DIVINERS, Morag muses on this possibility in her attitude to the beloved swallows, and comes to the conclusion that I have come to – so what? If we interpret birds and animals through our own perceptions, why, those are the only perceptions we have, and probably the birds and animals interpret <u>us</u> through their own types of perception, too. I so much like, also, your stories about your cat. I have been wanting to write a story about my cat, and for a long while I would do it as an animal fantasy, but just lately I am beginning to wonder if I won't simply tell the story as it happened – of course, I would have to portray her with "human" feelings, but really, people who feel that animals have no feelings recognizable by us are just mistaken, in my opinion, or they have never really observed animals very closely.

All in all, I thank you so much for the pleasure ENCHANTED SUMMER has given me. It is a book to cherish and re-read again and again.

My children and their respective mates and myself have decided to go to England for Christmas! A sudden and probably absurd decision, and we are all so excited about it. I have not been back since I returned permanently to Canada in 1973. There are many friends I'd like to see again. And of course, for Jocelyn and David it is a second home – they grew up there, and will remember Elm Cottage as their true childhood home. So we have all decided that we will not give each other presents this year. Instead, we will go to a few theatres, and to the carol service at Westminster Abbey, and we will visit old haunts – Trafalgar Square, the Tower, Hampstead Heath, all the places I took the kids when they were quite young, in 1962 when I went to London with them after separating from my husband. The kids, of course, have many friends in England. We will, for the first time ever, go out for Christmas dinner to a restaurant – it will be very different from Christmas at home, and one would not want to do it every year, but if we are all together, it will still be Christmas for us. I hope the weather is fairly good, but even if it isn't, I think it will be a good and interesting time.

I have now shut up my cottage for the winter, as the weather had begun to be too cold for enjoyment out there, so I'm back at home now. The winter season, as usual, promises to be busy, but I'm trying not to take on too many commitments. I need time to think about what I want to write next – it is still so vague and unformed in my mind, but perhaps it will come.

I hope things are well with you. And again — thanks
so much.

Love,

[signed] Margaret

p.s. How fortunate you are to have Joyce Marshall
translate ENCHANTED SUMMER! She must be one of the finest
translators we have. By the way, Le Cercle du Livre de France
in Montreal is bringing out a translation of THE STONE ANGEL
— in fact, I believe it is out now. Translation was one by
Claire Martin — I felt honoured to have such a translator. THE
DIVINERS is being translated into French by the daughter of M.
& Mme. Tisseyre of Le Cercle — perhaps you know them. I am
very pleased.

Your archeological tour in Greece resembles mine, about
twelve years ago, to the smallest detail.

Dear Margaret,

This morning of election day in Quebec I feel very
nervous, nevertheless wish to "converse" with you ... in a sense
I, too, had been waiting to read your very rich collection of
essays before writing to say my thanks for the gift of the book
and for the warm dedication. I am not quite finished yet, not
from lack of interest, far from it, but I have had too much to
do lately and have begun to feel very tired. I was very much
taken by your African stories or essays — I notice that you
built your essays with character, background ... very much in
the same way as one writes a good story; I proceeded almost
in the same way, when, years and years ago, I wrote feature
articles for <u>le Bulletin des Agriculteurs</u>. I knew little yet about
your African experience so this was all very interesting to me.
How quickly and early you became a good writer. One might
almost say that you have always been a good writer, from the
moment you started. I remember such groping, in my case.

You are also, as it seems, equally at ease in this genre as in fiction.

Your lovely letter, like the preceding ones, pleased me greatly. What I particularly enjoy in your letter writing is that it reveals you in your most natural self, in your daily behavior, one might say. I am glad to hear that you and your close-knit little tribe will journey to England and spend Christmas there. I spent two Christmas days in England in my life, and although I was wretchedly lonely – this being a time of my life when I was very much alone – I remember a sort of atmosphere of childlike wonder around me, as if Christmas in a way belongs particularly to the English. And maybe it does. I wish you all a very pleasant stay in the "sceptered isles". But return without fail to this country which would miss you terribly if you should stay away too long. I read your words of appreciation of <u>Enchanted Summer</u> with joy.

With fond regards,
Gabrielle

Dear Gabrielle:

It has been three months since I received your letter, and I hope you will forgive my long silence, partly owing to the fact that when I arrived back from England, I collected <u>one huge cardboard box</u> full of mail from the post office, and it has taken me more than a month to work through all the business letters, requests for help with theses, requests to come and speak here and there, and so on and on.

I do hope you are not feeling as tired as you were when you last wrote. It is difficult not to work too hard. Please take care – this is not an admonition, merely an expression of concern and affection.

When you last wrote, it was the eve of the Quebec elections.* I don't even presume to make any comments – I have not the right. I do feel, however, that Levesque is a man of integrity. I wish with all my heart that in Anglophone Canada (and yes, in the prairies which you and I both love so

---

* The historic Quebec provincial election of 16 November 1976 brought the first Parti Québécois government into power and made Quebec sovereignty a major political issue in Canada. René Lévesque was party leader, premier, and a potent force for Quebec nationalism.

much) that more people could have realized, really realized, long ago, the way in which many people in Quebec feel about their history, their language, their heritage, their identity. I only pray (and I use that word advisedly) that it may not be too late. I have never been in the slightest doubt about how Francophone Canadians feel about their language. It is the same way I feel about mine, even though for me, as for millions of Canadians not of English background, it was not the language of my ancestors. But I never knew Gaelic (or as Scots say, "had the Gaelic"); English is my birth tongue, and I love it. And yet I am always aware of the irony . . here I am, writing to you in my language, not in yours. I am as much to blame as any other "Anglo". The ideal would be for me to write to you in English, and for you to reply in French. And you could do it, that way, with full and complete understanding, but I could not. And yet I feel — it may be too late for me (and for all those middleaged civil servants taking crash courses in French), but surely we should begin with the children? A family irony of mine . . my daughter, educated in England, is pretty fluent in French. But surely primary school is the place to begin, and not from duty, but from a desire to know one another. Also, I believe that translations of books, from English into French, and from French into English, is one area which can help. I know that some of the younger Quebec writers aren't anxious to have their books translated, but one can hope they may change their minds, ultimately. I believe that, national considerations not withstanding, writers should be as widely read as possible. When I think that without translations, to speak realistically, I would have been deprived of your work, and of the work of so many others, it doesn't bear thinking about. And there are so many translations yet to be done, both ways. I have been so encouraged by the fact that Le Cercle du Livre de France has now put out my novel THE STONE ANGEL in a translation done by Claire Martin. They will be publishing THE DIVINERS in a translation done by the daughter of M. and Mme. Tisseyre. Well, I have wandered somewhat from what I began to speak about.

There are times when I find I cannot think too long at once about all the problems which beset us. One turns, as you did in ENCHANTED SUMMER, to things which are simple (and enormously complex as well) and beautiful and perhaps joyful. Also, to the humorous stories . . and my life seems to abound in these, thank God. It abounds in lots of other things as well, but I really do believe that laughter is a kind of gift of grace ... I mean laughter that is warm, of course, not malicious (but that isn't true laughter, is it?). So I would like to tell you a few stories, true ones, which have happened to me recently. Cheering Tales For Winter Reading.

The first is a very moving one, or was to me. When I arrived in England (and yes, my children and I did have a good visit there; we stayed with various friends and we met for Christmas and on a few other occasions) the friend in London with whom I was staying* asked me if by any chance I would like to attend a concert of Christmas carols given by the Royal Choral Society in the Albert Hall. She knew a woman, who was in the Society, and could get two tickets. My friend is a Canadian, a long ago prairie person who worked many years with the CBC with Andrew Allan and on the great Stage radio series, and who now lives and teaches in England. She was a bit unsure about the concert . . she herself isn't all that enchanted by carols, and she did not know how I would feel. I said YES YES PLEASE! I love carols, in very many ways . . partly a remembrance of childhood; partly the pure beauty of the songs; partly as a joyful kind of worship. So we went to the Albert Hall. A freezing night, and the bus took forever to get there. But, Gabrielle, it was fantastic! That great hall was absolutely packed . . it must hold <u>thousands</u>. Many of the

---

* The woman is most likely Alice Frick, a CBC stalwart. She retired to England and was a good friend of Margaret Laurence until her death.

people there had obviously been going to these carol services for years, because the family behind us (who had no doubt all been in their local church choir for a long time) were singing so well, in parts . . descant, the whole thing. What I should explain is that some of the carols were sung by the Choral Society by themselves, beautifully, the lesser known carols, but for the old and beloved and wellknown carols, the audience was invited to rise and sing. Hark the Herald Angels Sing. Once In Royal David's City. The First Noel. It Came Upon A Midnight Clear. Are the words really as beautiful and as moving as I think, or do I invest them with all the emotional impact of a lifetime? I don't think it matters. That vast audience, me included, rose and sang our hearts out. I could hardly see the words because of my tears, but that was all right . . I knew the words anyway. I thought of the hymn we call Old Hundred . . <u>All people that on earth do dwell/ Sing to the Lord with joyful voice…</u>

It was one of the most moving experiences I have ever had.

Dare we now go from the sublime to the ridiculous? Why not? The humorous is sublime too in its own way, or so I believe. Of course, if one was doing this in a novel or a story, one would have to make the appropriate transitions, or at least try to interweave the varying tones in ways that would not work to the detriment of either. However, this is a letter to a friend, and you will be able to make the transition.

Just after I returned home, early in January, a village man named Clayton Ridpath phoned me up and said that he was in charge of the local Lakefield Chamber of Commerce float which would be in the parade for the Kawartha Kup (yes, that is how they spell it) Races, which are snowmobile races held every year at a nearby village, Lindsay. He thought it would be a great idea to have a different kind of float this year, and he proposed to have a village float with the slogan, LAKEFIELD, LITERARY CAPITAL OF THE KAWARTHAS. (The Kawarthas being all the lakes hereabouts, and the general region being a tourist area in summer). I said I thought that was a fine idea. He said could he come over and discuss it. I said Of Course. So he did come, and told me his plans. The float was to include Colonel Sam Strickland who settled here in the 1840's, his famous sisters, Susanna Moodie and the immortal Catherine Parr Traill, and several others, and ... me. Well, heavenly days, I felt a bit inadequate to the distinguished company, but let it pass. Clayton said that High School kids would take the part of all these literary figures, and would be suitably costumed in clothes of the period, borrowed from a local theatre group. I said that the kid who took my part should be suitably and warmly clad in slacks, sweater and plaid shirt, my working uniform. Well, the great day arrived. I went out with my nextdoor neighbor, as the float was to run through the village in the afternoon before being taken to Lindsay for the grand parade at night. And sure enough, there it was, contained on a huge truck from Kingdon Lumber, driven by my neighbor's son Neal. On the float there were many small spruce trees, a log cabin, the High School kids (appropriately garbed) in the roles of Col. Sam, Catherine, Susanna, etc, and at the back of the float there was a desk, with some of my books, and a young girl (labelled Margaret Laurence) clad in A BRIGHT BLUE SNOWMOBILE SUIT! The kids from the High School, of course, knew me, and so we waved and yelled back and forth as the float went by! My neighbor and I were laughing so hard we found it difficult to speak. The kids thought it was great! The follow-up was that our Lakefield float won the prize at Lindsay that evening. Also, the local paper, The Lakefield Leader (which is a really good little local paper, run by a young new owner . . two years now . . and staffed by keen young people whose enthusiasm often is greater than their accuracy) reported the float, but got the slogan a bit wrong. Fortunately, they also printed a picture, which showed the slogan LAKEFIELD, LITERARY CAPITAL OF THE KAWARTHAS. But in the report, the slogan was described as . . (this is my punch line) . . LAKEFIELD, LITERARY CAPITAL OF THE WORLD.

Well, Gabrielle, the local newspaper people have done much blushing since then, but it has been a source of a lot of innocent merriment among us locals. I think I am beginning to feel like a villager, and to be accepted as such, and that feels good. We call each other by first names, and I like that.

I hope you are all right, despite all the difficulties of the world in which we live, and one's individual difficulties.

Love, and God bless –
[signed] Margaret

Dear Margaret,

I'm thoroughly ashamed for not having answered
before your so very good letter of many months ago. I moved
early, this year, to my summer cottage and trouble just about
rained on me without pause. I lacked water three or four
times, my telephone was continually out of order – they
don't care about little country lines such as ours – I had an
invasion of flying ants – the worst possible creatures. I do
believe that the last creatures to remain alive on this Earth,
should there be a cataclysm, will be insects. They have a
will to live, that I find terrifying. Anyhow I had to send for
an exterminator from Quebec, empty all the closets, the
cupboards, leave the house, settle at my neighbor's for two
days, while the exterminator, a young man on high heels,
was to go over the house. Well, in two hours he had spread
a little powdered poison all along the plinths, which I could
have done myself easily, and held his hand for a cheque for
$250.00. And there are still ants about. Not quite as much.
Perhaps they are the last survivors. In the midst of all this I
received the last proofs of my next book, Garden in the Wind,

translated by Alan Brown (by the way, isn't [it] wonderful that Joyce Marshall won the great prize for translation this year!*) and by then I was so stupefied and overtired that I could have thrown the old batch in my wood stove.

Still, is it not strange, when evening comes, when dusk is falling and the last robins are looking for another worm yet on my lawn, when I sit at my bay window and see the peace and harmony and quiet joy of living all around me, would you believe it, for a while I forget all my troubles at keeping house, I rock slowly as I look at the powerful river, the superb hills and the frail silhouette of my robin all alone in the gathering dark. Ah, such beauty! How is it that our hearts are so seldom free to take it all in! So much of our life is fight, fight, fight.

And I dare not mention to you – not yet – what is the most painful point to me at this time: the politics of Quebec. Yes, of course, some of it is good. We had to have a change. But I detect such arrogance, such tyranny already and, worst of all, the intolerance which often goes with a certain form of incorruptibility. I detect so much of the wrongs I have known all too well in my childhood and youth, I detect

* Joyce Marshall won the Canada Council Translation Prize for 1976 for *Enchanted Summer (Cet été qui chantait)*.

too much of this to live now in hope and fervent expectation, as one should. Of course, the ship can still straighten itself. But words now, I'm afraid, are of no avail. Except, coming from you and the generous group you adhere to and from our English speaking brothers and allies. There you see: "English" has come under my pen instead of, as it should be, "Canadian friends".

Besides, just now, I can do no more than try to recuperate and meditate in silence.

Please excuse my long delay in writing to you. There is much more, much more that I would like to say. Perhaps I'll come back to you again one of these days, soon. Meantime, enjoy your cabin, your delightful river which you have shared so lovingly with us all in your great Diviners.

With fond regards
Gabrielle

Dear Gabrielle,

Thanks so much for your letter. I am so sorry to hear about all your difficulties at your summer home. I know the trials of having the telephone go off – it happens at my summer cottage, it seems, after every storm, when branches blow against the lines. However, Bell is pretty good at getting service restored. I've never had a plague of flying ants, however – how <u>awful</u>. And for the exterminator to demand a payment like that after doing so little – it's adding insult to injury! I do hope the little brutes have now disappeared.

Yes, Quebec. It seems that everyone is terribly concerned and indeed heartbroken, but it is so difficult to know what to do. I myself feel that the views of many anglophone Canadians are not being adequately or even accurately presented to the Quebec people by the federal government. To express, as I and many many of my friends do, the passionate hope that this country may remain <u>one</u>, does not imply a faith in the status quo, of course, and I wish that this could be communicated. I am sure we need a new constitution and have needed one for a long time. The talk of "repatriating" the constitution* seems to me to be an exercise in futility – all we really need to do is to announce that our constitution is our country's business and ours alone. I expect Britain would be quite glad to be rid of it, but in any event, what could Britain do even if some diehard imperialists there disapproved? Nothing, obviously. Gary Geddes, poet and editor, is putting together a collection of essays etc on the whole question, and hopes to put it out in both English and French. I can't believe it will do much good, actually, but one must keep on trying to communicate. I enclose a copy of the essay I am contributing.** I found it very hard to write, and although I rewrote it about 10 times I am still not too happy with it. It is quite emotional, but how can one write about this subject without being emotional? I hope you do not mind that I have mentioned you, with great respect, in the essay.

It was marvellous that Joyce Marshall received the translator's award! I was just delighted. I'm so glad that you have a new book coming out. Is it translated by Joyce, as

---

* The Constitution was "patriated" from Britain on 17 April 1982 (including a Canadian Charter of Rights and Freedoms, among other provisions) without the consent of the Quebec legislature, but the Supreme Court subsequently ruled that the Constitution, respecting Canada's laws and conventions, was in force throughout Canada.

** "Listen, Just Listen," in *Divided We Stand*, ed. Gary Geddes (Toronto: Peter Martin, 1977).

well? I see that the English edition has been announced in McClelland & Stewart's fall list.

After travelling, it seems, all spring (to Vancouver – Simon Fraser University; Fredericton – conference; Saskatoon – writers' workshop; etc), at last I am out at my cottage. What a relief to be here! I am in future going to refuse all invitations to conferences etc – I shall never get back to writing unless I allow myself the time and space to meditate upon it. The river is beautiful; the baby swallows have just hatched and are already learning to fly; my little godson next door is a year old and we have erected a fence around both properties in order to protect him – he is, of course, fearless and we worry about the river. My brother and his family from Alberta will be with me for most of July, which will be a joy.

Take care, and let us try to be of good heart, although it is very difficult just now.

Love,

[signed] Margaret

Dear Margaret,

Just a word to let you know that I have received
your very good letter and your equally very good essay. It is
emotional, yes, but I agree with you, it cannot be otherwise.
How are we to write about our country, at this hour, if not
with our sorrowful hearts, our pain and regrets, perhaps. I
know I could only shed tears, at this moment. But my task
might be harder even than yours, for it is my side of our
people that I would have to move, to convince, and they too
being in a most excited frame of mind, I could hardly get to
them. So you are right or your friend Rudy* is when he says:
Just listen. It is a time indeed for silence, meditation, or, if
words it must be, let them be of friendship and understanding.

I was moved by your little paragraph on me, and how
deftly you brought it in. I, too, am honoured to be your friend.

---

* Perhaps the novelist Rudy Wiebe.

Let us not lose heart and let us continue, each according to his way, toward one another, even under dark skies.

Affectionately
Gabrielle

[appended note]

I have sometimes wondered, indeed, at your great understanding and compassion – you, of Scottish, Celtic, Irish descent – for Riel and Dumont and their people. Yet, I, in my next book, <u>Garden in the Wind</u>, I express, in my way, something of the same compassion for "our" immigrants, a Chinaman lost in the vastness of Saskatchewan, an old Ukrainian woman, at the end of the world, tending the last garden of her life. Perhaps we should congratulate one another on having learned that to become a writer – a genuine writer – is to do just that: embrace all variety into one ring of suffering humanity.

Alas, so few are ready yet to see that.

Gabrielle

Dear Gabrielle:

I feel badly at having taken so long to write to thank you for GARDEN IN THE WIND, which I read in the summer while I was at my cottage. How incredibly you have found your way into the minds and hearts of the people in the stories! Yes, it is something we have to try to do, and when it is people of very different backgrounds and cultures with whom we are dealing, it takes a very special leap of the imagination. I found all four stories so very moving in so many ways. First, of course, they're profoundly moving because you do lead the reader into the hearts of your characters, and we feel <u>with</u> them. And secondly because so much of the stories' content reminds me of my own prairie days. Like all prairie towns, mine also had a Chinese restaurant, and I can remember the days when no Chinese wives or children were there – only later on did I realize how terribly lonely it must have been for those men. Lee Ling, the proprietor of the first Chinese café in my town, was a truly wonderful man ... kindly to all children, as I recall well. My father always did his legal business, and every Christmas Lee would give our family a turkey, a box of chocolates and a box of lichee nuts. After my father died, Lee continued to give our family those Christmas gifts, every year until Lee himself died. I have always found that very remarkable. Your story of the Doukobors I found fascinating ... there is a kind of Old Testament prophet feeling about those people. Oddly, I had just finished reading THE DOUKOBORS, by George Woodcock and Ivan Avakumovic shortly before I read your story, so it had a special dimension for me. I loved "Tramp At The Door" . . the reader knowing all along the true state of affairs and yet realizing more and more the real truth that the mother comes to see only at the end. Perhaps the title story moved me most of all – one has often thought how lonely and yet how incredibly persevering must have been all those women like Marta, living out of their language areas, often with husbands grown despairing or numb, seeing their children move out, move on. To me, you have captured all this perfectly through Marta's eyes. Anyway, many many thanks for having written these beautiful stories.

I am trying to feel and think my way into another novel ... how slow the process often seems. One must be patient, and make a space in one's life so as to be able to find, gradually, what it is that one is perhaps being given to do with the writing. Often this is difficult . . I read somewhere this summer that all too often the <u>important</u> gives way to the <u>urgent</u>. This strikes me as true, and yet it is so hard to avoid it. I'm not doing any more travelling about, readings, seminars, lectures, etc. I did have a restful summer and did a lot of reading and thinking. I moved back from the cottage after Thanksgiving . . it was getting too cold to be there. I miss looking out at the river, but I do love my Lakefield house, too.

Again, thanks and love,

[signed] Margaret

Dear Gabrielle:

This will be a brief letter, as I have a horrifying stack of business letters to catch up on. But before I tackle them, I did want to write and tell you how wonderful it was to meet at last!* I only wish we had had more time, but at least it was so good actually to be able to talk for awhile. I would so much like to visit you some time. Would there be any chance of persuading you to visit me?

I was so amused to learn that we had received letters from the same students! Teachers, however, really should know better than to advise their young charges to write to authors with all kinds of complicated requests. One begins to feel like an agency.

I had a lovely trip home on the train. One realizes, going across the prairies by rail, what a huge country this is. I covered only about half of it, in terms of miles, and yet it

---

* February 1978 in Calgary. Both authors, among others, attended a conference organized by Malcolm Ross and Jack McClelland. One of the purposes of the conference was to announce a list of the 100 "best" Canadian novels as chosen by teachers and critics in a secret ballot. Margaret Laurence's *The Stone Angel* was chosen #1. See Robert Lecker's *Making It Real: The Canonization of English-Canadian Literature* (Toronto: House of Anansi, 1995).

---

took nearly 2 days and 2 nights. Also, although the prairies in winter may be difficult to cope with, how incredibly beautiful they are! And, of course, not empty at all, as non-prairie people envisage them to be. I wonder how all the wild birds survive – dried berries left on bushes? On the way out, near Maple Creek, I saw two small antelope standing near the tracks – my Calgary nephew told me these are "pronghorns", the fastest animals on earth, he says. The cheetah, he informed me, is faster in short stretches but the pronghorn can keep up speed for long distances. I love facts like that! On the way home, I looked out at dusk, and there was a prairie jackrabbit in all his winter white, bounding across a field. He stopped and looked at the train, and became almost invisible against the snow. I hadn't seen a prairie jackrabbit in years and years.

The next time I write it will be a proper letter. But I just wanted to get a note off to you.

With love,
[signed] Margaret

Dear Margaret,

I wonder what is a "proper letter" in your mind. Your
last one to me is a delight. You took me along with [you] on
the long train journey. You made me see through your eyes the
endless country, the deep sky the two of us love so much. You
made me see the winter clad jack rabbit. I hadn't seen one for
years and years. Just as you. And the pronghorns or antelope.
This gracious animal I never saw except in pictures. You have
over me a great advantage, dear Margaret. You can write to
me in your superb English, so alive and rich. If only I could
write to you in French. Still, never mind! We have been able
to reach to [one] another beautifully across what is called the
language barrier and which is not so much a barrier after all,
when people really wish to meet.

Jack* had been right about the Calgary air. And
what a sky! I had forgotten that it could be so high, so blue,
so uplifting. Anyhow, I breathed much more easily there. The
altitude may have helped. Apparently it's just the right altitude
in Calgary for me according to what several doctors in France

---

* Jack McClelland of McClelland and Stewart.

prescribed for me: around three thousand feet. I felt better and better. Was it the climate? Or the joy of coming out of my captivity and meeting so many fascinating, stimulating people and who seemed to love me – how have I come to deserve this affection I read in quite a few people's eyes and which filled me with wonder? It was all together too short, of course, but so intense, so much worthwhile.

Upon returning to Quebec though, all my woes returned to me. As in that terrible add [sic] in favour of I know not which medicine, my nose felt stuffy, my throat ached, my eyes cried, my chest heaved and I was miserable. I looked up at the sky. And no wonder I felt miserable! It was low, filled with dirt, murky. How did we humans allow ourselves to sink into that sort of non-living we call life. It's all our fault in a sense. But how can we spend our life fighting so much wrong everywhere.

To have met you in the flesh remains the great reward of the journey. Now I see in the Montreal Star a friend sent me that <u>The Stone Angel</u> came first in both lists, the ten and the hundred best novels.* And I am so glad. I had no time

---

*The ballot and the discussion on it are included in *Taking Stock: The Calgary Conference on the Canadian Novel,* ed. Charles R. Steele and Hallvard Dahlie (Toronto: ECW Press, 1982). On List A, "the most 'important' one hundred works of fiction," *The Tin Flute* is first on the list. On List B, "the most 'important' ten novels," *The Tin Flute* is fifth on the list and *The Stone Angel* is first.

to ask you what you thought of the big literary hunt. One thing troubles me, or amuses me perhaps: it is to see the great number of writers from McClelland in that list. Or is it after all natural seeing Jack publishes so many Canadian writers?

Do look after yourself and live a happy life in as much as you can.

Affectionately
Gabrielle

Dear Gabrielle:

I do feel ashamed that it has taken me so long
to answer your last letter, and also so long to write and
CONGRATULATE YOU ON WINNING THE GOVERNOR GENERAL'S
AWARD FOR YOUR LAST BOOK!!! I was delighted. Do you know
when we may look forward to an English translation? It is
at times like this that I feel the worst at not being able to
read French. The winner in the English language for fiction
was Timothy Findley's novel, THE WARS. I was chairman of
the fiction committee, and it was nice that the committee's
decision was unanimous. It's a splendid novel. Of course the
press gave its usual minimal coverage to the event. I think the
Canada Council must also take some responsibility, too, for
making the announcements so late. But it always annoys me
to see the very little bit of publicity the Governor-General's
Awards get – one would hope that such an award might
increase the sales of the books, but how can it if no one hears
of it? In our local Peterborough paper, the only mention of
the awards was a brief report stating that one of the French-

Canadian writers had refused his award,* a piece of reporting that says much about the Peterborough Examiner, none of it good!

It was wonderful to meet you in Calgary in February, at last! I feared that McClelland was pressuring you to do too much, however, and I was worried that you would be exhausted when you got home. The whole question of the literary lists seemed to me to have been played up far too much. Malcolm Ross** had intended that the lists would be announced at the beginning of the conference, not the end, and that they would serve only as a talking point – they weren't intended to be definitive lists in any way. However, this was mis-interpreted by the media, and Malcolm came in for a lot of criticism, and I was terribly sorry about that, as it really hurt him. Adele Wiseman*** and I, who have been friends of Malcolm for many years, did what we could to correct the impression here.

I am out at my cottage now, looking at the beloved river, and I wonder if you are now at your summer place, overlooking your beloved river.

---

* Michel Garneau refused his award in 1977.
** A literary critic and a major figure in twentieth-century Canadian culture, Malcolm Ross was Margaret Laurence's and Adele Wiseman's professor at the University of Manitoba. He was the founding editor of the New Canadian Library.
*** A lifelong close friend of Margaret Laurence, Adele Wiseman was born in Winnipeg in 1928. Her novel, *The Sacrifice*, won the Governor-General's award for fiction in 1956. She died in Toronto in 1992.

I have been here for less than a month and can hardly believe it is July already. I don't think the tensions of the winter have quite dropped away from me yet, but each day I feel a little calmer and more relaxed. When I'm too busy, as I always seem to be in the winter, I find I can't do any real thinking and hence no real writing. These summers are so important to me.

A National Film Board crew spent 3 days with me (not staying at my house, thank goodness, but they were there at my Lakefield house 8 hours a day for the 3 days). They are doing a half-hour documentary on me. They are, I am happy to say, paying me for participating. It was an odd experience — so much of the time was taken up with their setting up the lights and various exotic equipment. Those cameras frighten me, but I guess I managed to get through the interview without appearing too nervous. They went out to my old home town of Neepawa and apparently interviewed a lot of people there — I wonder what they said about me!! It always seems odd to me that a film crew needs thousands of feet of film, and hours of filming, to produce half an hour of finished film. How strange it would be if writers felt they had to do a first draft of about 16 times the length of the finished manuscript.

The baby swallows are about to take off from the nests, and the parent birds are desperately busy trying to lure the babies into flight. They are chattering madly to one another outside my windows right now. They are such conscientious parents. The babies are usually out by now – it was a very late spring here this year. Sometimes if the little ones are out of the nest early enough, the swallows have two broods in a year.

A very happy thing happened to me recently. The story goes back 18 years to the time when we lived in Vancouver. At that time I attended the Unitarian church, and once when some parents objected (!) to the Christmas story being told to the Sunday school children because the angels really hadn't been flying around in the sky, I was very upset and said I would not want my own young children to be deprived of that most important part of their heritage. I therefore offered to write a version of the story for use with very small children. I did so, and the story was used in the Sunday school. When I left Vancouver, I mislaid the story and thought it was gone forever. Then, last winter I was having dinner at some friends' home, and one of the guests was a woman from Vancouver who was a Unitarian. She asked me if I remembered the story, and I said certainly I did, but I had lost my copy years ago. To my astonishment, she told me the story is still being used in the Unitarian Sunday school! She subsequently sent me a copy, so it returned to me after 18 years. I rewrote it very slightly, and then mentioned it (very timidly) to a friend of mine, Helen Lucas, who is a very fine artist. She liked the version of the story of the baby Jesus, and said that it might be that she would be moved to do some illustrations. I had told her that I would like to see it come out as a little book, but only if the pictures were beautiful (I could just imagine a publisher ruining it by having illustrations in Walt Disney style!). She just phoned me last night to tell me she had seven illustrations, simple line drawings, white on an off-white background so that children could add the colours themselves! She is coming up here day after tomorrow to show them to me, and I am very excited, because I am sure I'll love them. Now if we can find a publisher to do a really lovely production job … well, we'll see.* But it seemed as though the story were meant to be brought out as a small book, as it returned to me in that quite unlikely way.

---

* The book was published as *A Christmas Birthday Story*, illus. Helen Lucas (Toronto: McClelland and Stewart, 1980).

I'll send this to your Quebec City address, and I hope someone will forward it if you are at your summer place.

Please take care, dear Gabrielle.

Love,

[signed] Margaret

Dear Margaret,

I thought you would be interested to see one of these cards* a Manitoban artist designed. I have to ask my forgiveness for having been so long to write you a word at least in answer to your lovely letter. I'm so glad to hear that you found this Christmas story of yours, apparently lost. What a piece of luck. I'm eager to read it. The trip to Calgary was tiring in a sense, but so rewarding in another and well worth the fatigue if only to afford a meeting with you … and a few other people I was eager to know. And then I discovered that the air at the foot of the mountains suited me and helped me greatly. Since [then] I have toyed with the idea of settling near Calgary – but I'm afraid I'd be lonely as a lost cat.

I hope this summer has been profitable and happy for you. It has been a miracle in a sense, hasn't [it], so warm, so vibrant, so long!

Love and my warmest wishes to you,
Gabrielle

* This letter is written on a card with a drawing of a church (Église Sainte-Marie de Toutes-Aides) by Manitoba artist Réal Bérard (St. Boniface: Les Éditions Nico).

Hollywood [Florida]

❡ February 7, 1979 ❡

Dear Margaret,

I've just received two advanced copies of my new book* and am sending you one right away. Some leaves may be stuck together … at least I found a few in that state. The book, I suppose, is too fresh from the oven. Also excuse the rough package. I had to make do with what I had under my hand.

Myself will be returning to Quebec fairly soon. In about a week or so. The climate has done me no good. I've had bad spells almost every night and I'm anxious to be treated by my own doctor. All those remedies I take to stop coughing are making me hazy in my mind, confused and forgetful. I hope you are well and as happy as possible. Looking forward to your beloved summer retreat!

I am besieged on all sides, Margaret and sometimes am afraid to lose bottom.

God bless you.

Yours with warm affection
Gabrielle

---

* *Ces enfants de ma vie (Children of My Heart).*

Dear Gabrielle:

I received your letter from Florida today. I am just
so terribly sorry you have been so unwell. I hope so much
that you will feel better when you get back home. All the
expressions of concern and sympathy seem to me to be such
helpless clichés and do not at all express the strength of my
true feelings of concern for you, and my sadness that you are
having such a difficult time. Please believe that I am thinking
of you and praying that you may soon feel much much better.

I am doing a strange thing with this letter – I am
making a carbon copy so that I can send one to Florida and
one to Quebec! I want to communicate with you as soon as
possible, hence the one to Florida. But just in case you decide
to return to Quebec sooner than in several weeks time, I want
to write there, as well, as I don't want to risk the possibility
of your not receiving this letter. (Of course, given our Post
Office, I suppose one always runs the risk!) So if you receive
two identical letters from me, you will understand why.

Thank you so very much for sending me a copy of
CHILDREN OF MY HEART. I have not yet received it, but will

be delighted to have it. In that connection, something has happened that I hope will please you. When I received your letter, I was on the point of writing to you! I had been sent a copy of CHILDREN OF MY HEART and had just finished reading it a few days ago. McClelland & Stewart had sent me a copy. I will be glad to have the two copies; the one you are sending me is the one I shall keep and cherish. The other I can lend to friends. I wanted to write right away and tell you how much I loved the book.

Justice was done when you were awarded the Governor General's award for the book in French. I think Alan Brown's translation must be a very faithful one, for the book seems – I don't quite know how to express this – it seems almost perfect, flawless. I was so moved by the stories of all the children, and by the portrayal of the young teacher, scarcely more than a child herself, trying to understand her charges, loving them, sometimes bewildered by them. I was in tears at many points throughout the story, especially when reading about the little Ukrainian boy with the lark's voice, and about Médéric ... that final tale I found so very moving and evocative. In the town where I grew up, there were one or two young men like that . . having to act so tough and yet being so unhappy within the confines of school, and happy only when in touch with the land and its creatures. How beautifully you have portrayed Médéric, and how delicately you have explored his feelings and those of the young teacher towards him. When I was a child, there was an isolated Ukrainian settlement somewhere near Riding Mountain (I have forgotten the name of the place, but on our way to Clear Lake we could see the onion spires of the Greek Orthodox church at a distance). The local legend was that the settlement had been started by a Hungarian nobleman who had come to Canada, bringing all the Ukrainian peasants and serfs from his old-country estate (the Ukraine then being part of the Austro-Hungarian empire). He had tried to impose a feudal system on "his" people, until they discovered that they did not need to be serfs of his in the new land. I wrote a story about this, when I was in college, long ago. Médéric's father might have been just such a man.

I can't begin to tell you how much I loved CHILDREN OF MY HEART. There is something so crystal-clear and flowing and pure about your writing, like a mountain stream. And it is the quality of gentleness and tenderness in it, combined with the knowledge of life's pain and sadness, that speak to me.

Thank you for having written this book, dear Gabrielle, and for being so very thoughtful as to send me a copy.

My writing is beginning again, but slowly. Not, this time, fiction, but something else – I don't know yet how it will turn out. I have also a small book . . a children's story . . coming out this year . . not the Nativity story, which will come out next year, but rather like a children's science fiction story! At least, it involves a kind of magic time-travel.

We have a lot of snow here, and in the village (unlike Toronto) the snow is <u>real</u> snow . . white and untouched in many places. I love it. The only things I don't care for are the icy streets and the wind, but we have had neither, just lately. The snow is that hard-packed stuff that crunches under one's boots, like prairie snow.

My thoughts and prayers are with you, and I am hoping so much that soon you will feel greatly improved.

God bless, and much love,
[signed] Margaret

Dear Margaret,

I received your so friendly letter here just in time, before leaving, this coming Thursday, and I was made happy by it, by your concern over me, by your lovely appreciation of my book. I am so pleased that you like it. Thanks for sending me this letter in Florida. Somehow it will make my trip home more pleasant. It is as if I will have company all the way home.

Bless your kind heart.

Gabrielle

I presume your phone number is private. Would you let me know it, Margaret? Some day I may feel a great need to talk with you.

G.

Dear Gabrielle:

A brief note. I'm so glad you received my letter while you were in Florida. I hope you had a good journey home, and that you are feeling a bit better. My phone numbers are: home . . (705) –652-8753; cottage . . (705) –745-4009. I did finally have to get unlisted numbers, because so many people phoned me and wanted me to get their manuscripts published for them, and that kind of thing.

I have just got home after a week away, during which time I spent two days at St. Andrew's College in Aurora, Ontario . . a private boys' school (high school). I was exhausted when I finished, as I had NINE sessions with students of various grades, in groups of 25 to about 50 . . in two days! However, the boys were enthusiastic and bright, so I enjoyed it as well. My father attended that school before World War One, and they very kindly looked up the old records of his attendance . . I was astonished that the old records still existed. I learned that he had kept his old school informed about some events in his life, and there was one entry that moved me very much . . "July 18/26 . . birth of a daughter, Jean Margaret". He must have been very pleased at my birth, to inform his old high school! He died when I was only nine, so I felt somehow that seeing the old record was like a kind of message all across those years.

Oh, I do hope so much that you are feeling better, Gabrielle.

With love,
[signed] Margaret

[handwritten]

Dear Gabrielle –

      I hope you will forgive me for not having written to you for some time. I am trying to start a new book, but oh! It is so difficult – the business letters pour in; and now I have to go to Toronto to publicize this new little book.

      I think of you so much, and wonder how you are.

      I hope this book gives you some pleasure. The houses are all taken from Lakefield houses! I love the pictures.

Much love to you,

Margaret

Dear Margaret,

On my returning home from a month's stay at the
hospital for a myocardio infarct, I found your delightful little
book awaiting me. Strangely, I too am publishing a story for
the young this year. It will come out in a few weeks and I
will hasten to have a copy sent to you. Mine is about a very
motherly cat called Courte-Queue.

I have a feeling that you and I have been worn out
far more by the business letter and all the demands on us than
by our own work. It seems to me there must have been a time
when writers wrote their books and were otherwise left alone.

So do be careful and do not overtax yourself. You are
far younger than I and in good health – so I hope. Still the
demands on your time and strength are incessant and much
more than a human being can sustain. And where are we to
find the time to dream our dreams out of which come out our
books?

I am dreadfully weak, cannot sustain an effort more
than a few minutes. I try my best to answer at least my best
friends.

Do not make excuses for not having written for quite a long time. As a matter of fact, I'm the one who owe[s] you a letter. And yours are always so much better than mine.

I'll tell you about your dear little book soon, I hope. Yes, the pictures are charming.

Affectionately yours
Gabrielle

[handwritten]

Dear Gabrielle –

A proper letter follows. And thank you for your letter. About my other little book,* this one was intended for beginning readers of 5 & 6 years old. The record was made only for promotion – it isn't being sold. But the tune of the song is <u>my</u> tune – wow!

I am really so delighted & amused by the fact that this tiny record was made. Ann Blades is a young B.C. artist, & I love her work.

For my own work, that is, to try to write a novel, I feel anxious, worried, depressed. But at least these kids' books are a kind of gift. A sort of grace given.

Much love,
Margaret

---

*Six Darn Cows, illus. Ann Blades (Toronto: James Lorimer, 1979).

Dear Margaret,

I'm in love with your the <u>Olden days coat</u>. It is a charming story and so well told.

The illustrations accompanying my Courte-Queue are not as authentic as yours. They are the work of a young Frenchman just come to this country,[*] and his picture of people and interiors are more French than Canadian. Being sick, I could not attend to everything.

Still I hope you will derive some pleasure out of my little book.

Yours is really enchanting.

Affectionately
Gabrielle

---

[*] François Olivier.

Dear Gabrielle:

I feel so badly that it has taken me so long to thank you for your children's book, Courte Queue. Much belatedly, thanks so very much. I wanted to wait until I could get my daughter to translate it for me. This she did at Christmas when I was in Toronto. I was back home in Lakefield only a few days when my dearest friend, Adele Wiseman, phoned to say that her mother had died. I went into Toronto immediately, and stayed until a few days ago, doing what I could to help. Adele's mother was a marvellous and very wise woman, who had a huge extended family group. She was almost like a mother to me, for the 33 years that Adele and I have been close friends. My own children always called her Bobba, and loved her as though she'd been their grandmother. She will be greatly missed not only by her own family but by so many of us.

I found your children's story very very moving indeed. Parts of it are very sad, but I think that children recognize sadness and need to become acquainted with it in books. I am sure all children are quite often sad, and can identify with those feelings. I think the mother cat's bravery and tenacity are marvellously portrayed. I also liked the illustrations – I can see what you mean about their seeming French rather than Canadian, but I think they are awfully well done.

I am trying so hard to get started at another novel. I hope I will be able to stay home and work now. (Not that I wasn't glad to go to Toronto to be with Adele – I was <u>very</u> glad and felt it was my privilege). During November and December, I had to go in often for publicity for my little kids' books. It seems that something is always coming up – in March I am giving a paper at a Royal Society symposium. Why did I ever agree?! Never mind – the ideas won't go away.

This is such a brief letter – forgive me. I do hope things are reasonably all right with you. I think of you so often.

Again, many thanks, and love,
[signed] Margaret

Dear Gabrielle:

It was wonderful to talk with you on the phone!
How glad I am that you called! I do so much hope the new
translation of The Tin Flute comes into being. I am, however,
distressed to think that someone holds the film rights forever
— are you sure nothing can be done? It seems just awful.
<u>Of course</u> I can understand why, years ago, you would have
signed such a contract. These film contracts are incredibly
complex. When I sold the film rights for A Jest Of God,
luckily I had an agent. I would have signed anything that gave
me $30,000 — a vast sum, even now, to me, and even more so
then when I was pretty broke.

I'm sending you a copy of Les Oracles (The
Diviners). It has turned out to be a very thick book . . more
than 500 pp . . in the French edition, so I am looking for a
book envelope large enough! The production job is very good,
and I am quite certain the translation is an excellent one. As I
think I told you, Michelle Robinson (the daughter of Michelle
and Pierre Tisseyre), who translated it, is a wonderful
young woman . . and she has taken all kinds of care with the

translation. It should really be Michelle who autographs it to you, not me. I have to admit, dear Gabrielle, when I wrote in the book for you, I was sorely tempted to cheat! The thought crossed my mind, briefly, that it would be nice to autograph it in French. But how could I? Obviously, by copying <u>your</u> inscription to me in Courte Queue!!! I almost instantly perceived, however, that this would not be an honourable thing to do!

My writing goes so slowly and so badly, of late. I have three times made a false start at a novel, and so far have torn up about 50 pp of handwriting. However, my handwriting is somewhat large and scrawling, so it isn't as much as it sounds. I am pretty sure there is a novel there, somewhere, if only I can find it .. or at least find my way into it. It has often been this way with me, but I tend to forget, and to think that it has never before been as difficult as this time. It does, though, in some ways, get more difficult each time. One must forget any potential readership, or the critics, or anyone except the characters themselves. This was easier some years ago than it is now. In a sense, it was easier to write when my books were relatively unknown. When people say to me (as they often do), "I'm just waiting for your next book," my heart positively sinks. I want to say to them, "Don't hold your breath while you're doing it, because it may be a long time." However, we go on in some way or another. It is a strange profession that we chose, Gabrielle . . or rather, that chose us.

I don't know at all if you would be interested, but I am also sending you two other things. One is a reprint, in The United Church Observer, of a dialogue-sermon I did with my old friend, Rev. Lois Wilson* at Chalmers United Church in Kingston, last year. We did a dialogue instead of having a sermon at a Sunday service. We spoke of things that we had often previously discussed. It was taped, and the United Church Observer reprinted it.** It does represent my true feelings, but, being a writer, and seeing it in print rather than having it as the spoken word, I look at it and think how inadequately I have expressed myself. I would like to take my parts and re-write them! Lois did much better because she is a minister and because she isn't as vague in her expression of some of these things as I think I am. However, you might be interested to see it. Incidentally, my friendship with Lois Wilson and her husband, Roy, both United Church ministers,

---

* Lois Wilson was the first woman to be elected Moderator of the United Church of Canada (1980) and later was appointed to the Canadian Senate (1998).
**The article was published in the February 1980 *Observer*, pp. 10–12. It was titled "Why pick on Margaret Laurence?" The novelist and victim of book-banners tells about the Christian faith that underlies her books. There were photos on page 10 and page 12.

goes back 35 years, to United College* days in Winnipeg. Lois and I were in the same year, Roy one year ahead. They both then went on to take Theology, after getting the B.A., and married shortly after they both graduated. Lois, however, did not become ordained until some years later, when her 4 children had all reached school age ... at that time, apparently, although the United Church had been ordaining women ministers for some time, they looked rather askance on married women ministers! However, Lois pressed on and has become something of a pioneer in her field. They are both wonderful people. We lost touch for many years, after college, and then I discovered them again when I returned to Canada in 1973. Life has taken us on very different paths, but we have ended up with so many of the same perceptions and beliefs.

The other thing I am sending is an interview in The Canadian Forum that I did with Hilda Kirkwood, a long-time board member of the Forum, and a woman who was reviewing my books enthusiastically when practically no one else here had noticed them! Again, it's an interview I'd like to re-write, but it does bring out some of my views and feelings. (For what

---

* Since 1967, the University of Winnipeg. The founding colleges, Manitoba College (1871) and Wesley College (1888) merged to form United College in 1938. Laurence graduated from United College in 1947.

they're worth).

Please take care, dear Gabrielle, and please know how cherished you are to so many of us.

Love,
[signed] Margaret

P.S. Good news . . Joyce Marshall will be coming to Trent University for the next academic year, as writer-in-residence. Trent is only about 2 miles from my house, so it will be lovely to be able to see her often. I had a long talk with her on the phone not long ago, as she wanted to hear about my experiences when I was writer-in-residence at Trent. I told her she had only one worry — she must try very hard not to be <u>too</u> conscientious!! I believe that a writer-in-residence should earn her or his salary, (and in this not all writers agree with me), but I know that my own tendency was . . as Joyce's will be . . to take on far too much and to become exhausted. However, Trent is a good university, and a <u>small</u> one . . and that is a blessing.

Dear Margaret,

I have received the two magazines – most interesting
– your good letter which I cherish as much as all the others
you have written to me, how can you write such pleasant
letters, find the proper tone so earthy, warm and easy, I
wonder! and finally, yesterday <u>Les Oracles</u>, a handsome
book even if it does not quite compare with the impressive
American edition. I have right away – before testing some
more – read the first page in French before comparing with
the original and was immediately taken up as if reading in the
original. Then I read the haunting songs at the end. You can
rest your mind, dear Marguerite, those are done with uncanny
feeling and talent. I almost found myself crying over the so
sad ballad; Piquette's song. The other test I made but perhaps
too quickly, I will do it at leisure little by little, is comparing
your colloquial with your translator's colloquial, that is I
didn't compare it yet, I just read a few paragraphs of hers
which at first glance I would say rings true [and] right and
seems just the sort of transposition that is needed here. Of
course it is a big book and to make sure that the translation

is perfectly good right through would take some time and is quite a task, but my feeling right now, after what I have seen, is that your book has not been betrayed. I have the feeling that the work has been done with love and a flair for the right kind of transposition which is after all very near creative talent itself. Later on I will let you know more about what I feel. On the whole I am impressed and very glad for you. I do hope that you will have in Quebec the readers you so rightly deserve. If they only come to you, then I know they will take to you.

I am trying to write something of a letter today, to make up for such a long silence on my part, as my right hand is a little less stiff, but I'm afraid it won't last long. This bout of arthritis is very severe and long.

Unfortunately – but it doesn't really matter to me anymore – it is only too true that I signed such a stupid contract with Hollywood some thirty-five years ago. I am left in the dark and have just learned by hearsay that the rights have been bought back and that there is talk of making a film. By whom, I don't even know. Jack McClelland once mentioned Nielsen but since I have heard neither from him nor from anybody else touching this matter. But who cares after all! Only one thing now is important to me: to finish the book I'm fighting my way through with poor hands, poor breath, poor heart. Yet the miracle may happen and I may give it my last efforts, which is a fine way, I feel, to come to a conclusion. Is the work worth all that much, I don't know, possibly not, probably not, but I don't care.

Pursue your own dear work, Margaret and do not despair. Of course it is more and more difficult as we go on. How could it be otherwise! In a sense, I am glad for Joyce, if it makes her happy to become a writer-in-residence. But who knows, timid as she is, she might do better work by herself in her small corner. Nothing else suits me now but my corner, if only my friends were not so far, and could come to me oftener.

I am running into a fourth page and now my hand will hardly move much further.

Don't tear up pages of your new book. Let them rest away from your eyes for some time. Somehow you might get a pleasant surprise if you look at them after a few months. Occasionally that has happened to me.

With affectionate wishes
Gabrielle

I like that face of yours on The Observer. It is a face, somehow, that speaks of a great storage of knowledge, from the mind and from the heart.

Again my affectionate thoughts.

G.

Dear Gabrielle:

I have thought of you so often this past summer, and have been meaning to write for ages. Now that I'm actually doing so, it's good to be able to send you the enclosed little book. There is a wonderful story about this book and how it came into being. It is always so good when one can tell a happy story, in this terrifying world of ours.

It began more than 20 years ago, when we lived in Vancouver.* My son was then 4 and my daughter 7. At that time, we attended the Unitarian Church, and our kids went to the Sunday School there. One Christmas I wrote a re-telling of the Nativity story, for use with small children. I wanted to tell it in such a way that small children would understand and be able to connect with. I really wanted to emphasize the birth of the beloved child into the loving family. Of course, I took some liberties with the story (such as saying Mary and Joseph didn't mind whether their baby turned out to be a boy or a girl! But that seemed so natural – I had one of each, after all, and it seemed to me that children of today would

---

* Margaret Laurence repeats the story she recounts in her letter of 2 July 1978.

relate to the concept of the <u>child</u> being wanted, whether boy or girl). Of course, many variations of the story have occurred for hundreds of years – in paintings, tales, carols – many of them with very little reference to the story as it is told in the gospels (e.g. the carol . . I Saw Three Ships Come Sailing In). Of course I took the main elements of the story from St. Matthew and St. Luke – but the two gospel stories differ quite a bit from one another, too.

When I left Vancouver in 1962, and went with my children to England, I somehow lost my only copy of the story. It remained lost to me for 15 years. Then, in the Christmas season of 1977, I was invited to the home of friends who live near Lakefield. There I met a woman who also lives near here. She asked me if I remembered my re-telling of the Nativity story, so many years before. I told her I certainly did, and that to my sorrow, I'd lost my only copy when I left Vancouver. Then – to my delight and astonishment – she told me that she and her husband and their children had lived in Vancouver during the years we were there, and she had a copy of the story, which she used to read to her children when they were young, each Christmas! Imagine! She sent me a copy of the story, and so it came home to me after so long. I thought this must mean something, so

I re-wrote the story slightly, and added to it a little, and then I asked the Toronto artist, Helen Lucas (whom I had recently met – another wonderful happenstance) if she would consider doing some pictures for it. She did, and we submitted it to Knopf and to McClelland & Stewart. Both accepted it, and the book you now see is the result! I am thrilled with it. I think Helen's pictures have exactly the love and tenderness – and yes, some humour, too – that I hoped to convey in the text. The picture of the infant Jesus is like a sunburst.

I do have very special feelings about this book. It does seem as though it was meant to be. The fact that it had been lost to me for so long, and that when I found it I had just met an artist whom I <u>knew</u> would be exactly the right person to create the pictures. The fact that Nonie Lyon, who returned the story to me, had lived in Vancouver at that time, had gone to the Unitarian Church (I had not met her in those days), had a copy, and had actually settled in the same part of Canada as myself, and the fact that mutual friends had asked us to their home on that day in the Christmas season! With my dour Protestant upbringing, I am not much of a believer in miracles, and yet – a number of small seeming miracles have indeed happened to me in my life, and I am grateful.

I sold my cottage this spring. Not because of financial need, but because it was getting to be a bit too much of a responsibility to have 2 places, and also because it had, I came to see, served its purpose in the 10 years I had it. I could not write there, now, because I think in my mind the river at that place was too much connected with the writing of <u>The Diviners.</u> The same river flows through this village, and is only half a block from my house, so I can see it any time, but from a different viewpoint. This seemed to be the right thing to do. I seemed to have a need to simplify my life. Goodness knows, it wasn't all that simple all summer — I had a steady stream of visitors. I enjoyed them very much, but didn't get much writing done. I still have not found my way into the novel I want to write. I think it will come, but when? Patience is difficult for me, and I am fed up with making false starts at it. This often depresses me, as does, greatly more so, the state of the world. Still, many good things do happen.

Dear Gabrielle, I hope and pray that your health has improved, and that you were able to spend the summer beside your river.

With love,
[signed] Margaret

Dear dear Gabrielle —

Please forgive me for my long silence. I have thought of you so very often, but have not written to you.

No excuse! I have spent the past two years in trying, without much success, to write the novel I have been attempting to do for so long. Maybe I will do it — maybe not. We will see. It has been a good time for me, in terms of my own life and friends and children, but not such a good time in terms of my work, which still seems to evade me, much as I try. I do not tell many people about this anguish, because they would not understand and because it is my own private concern. I can speak about it to Adele Wiseman, my dear and old friend, and my daughter Jocelyn, and very few others. Well, Gabrielle, I am trying and not giving up, and I am doing a lot of other things . . work with anti-nuclear groups, work with young children in enriched (?) programs here in my county, and so on and so on. I am not without work or without concerns. But my writing seems to puzzle and foil me. Perhaps it will work out . . I hope so. I seem to stand in need of grace. I feel, however, that the early church fathers (I would have liked the 'mothers' there, too) were right in saying despair was a deadly sin. I am not in despair, but I am not, either, seeming to be able to write as I would wish to. We will see. I read recently your book "The Fragile Lights of Earth" .. loved it; loved your early writings about the many peoples in the prairies; loved your humorous account of how you got the Prix Femina! Thanks so much for that book. I hope you are reasonably well and going on. I love you so much, always, for what you have given me in your writing, and I take courage from you.

Love, and blessings for the new year.

[signed] Margaret

✻ SELECTED BIBLIOGRAPHY ✻

This is a selection of books by and about Margaret Laurence and Gabrielle Roy. For a complete bibliography of books and articles by and about these two writers, please consult the University of Manitoba Press's website at www.umanitoba.ca/uofmpress.

Books by Margaret Laurence

A Tree for Poverty: Somali Poetry and Prose. Published for the British Protectorate of Somaliland, Nairobi: Eagle Press, 1954. Reprint, Dublin: Irish University Press and Hamilton: McMaster University Library Press, 1970.

This Side Jordan, 1960, Toronto: McClelland and Stewart; London: Macmillan; New York: St. Martin's Press.

The Tomorrow-Tamer and Other Stories, 1963, Toronto: McClelland and Stewart; London: Macmillan; New York: Knopf, 1964.

The Prophet's Camel Bell, 1963, Toronto: McClelland and Stewart; retitled *New Wind in a Dry Land,* 1964, New York: Knopf.

The Stone Angel, 1964, Toronto: McClelland and Stewart; London: Macmillan; New York: Knopf.

A Jest of God, 1966, Toronto: McClelland and Stewart; London: Macmillan; New York: Knopf; also *Rachel, Rachel,* 1966, New York: Knopf.

Long Drums and Cannons: Nigerian Dramatists and Novelists: 1952-1966, 1968, London: Macmillan; New York: Praeger, 1969.

The Fire-Dwellers, 1969, Toronto: McClelland and Stewart; London: Macmillan; New York: Knopf.

A Bird in the House, 1970, Toronto: McClelland and Stewart; London: Macmillan; New York: Knopf, 1970.

Jason's Quest [illustrated by Steffan Torell], 1970, Toronto: McClelland and Stewart; London: Macmillan; New York: Knopf.

The Diviners, 1974, Toronto: McClelland and Stewart; London: Macmillan; New York: Knopf.

Heart of a Stranger, 1976, Toronto: McClelland and Stewart.

Six Darn Cows [illustrated by Ann Blades], 1979, Toronto: James Lorimer.

The Olden Days Coat [illustrated by Muriel Wood], 1979, Toronto: McClelland and Stewart.

A Christmas Birthday Story [illustrated by Helen Lucas], 1982, Toronto: McClelland and Stewart.

Dance on the Earth: A Memoir, 1989, Toronto: McClelland and Stewart

Gunnars, Kristjana, ed. *Crossing The River: Essays in Honour of Margaret Laurence*. Winnipeg: Turnstone Press, 1988.

Hughes, Terrance Ryan. *Gabrielle Roy et Margaret Laurence: deux chemins, une recherche*. Saint-Boniface, Manitoba: Editions du Blé, 1987.

Kertzer, Jonathan. *"That House in Manawaka": Margaret Laurence's A Bird in the House*. Toronto: ECW Press, 1992.

Kertzer, J.M. *Margaret Laurence and Her Works*. Toronto: ECW Press, 1987.

King, James. *The Life of Margaret Laurence*. Toronto: A.A. Knopf Canada, 1997.

Lennox, John, ed. *Margaret Laurence-Al Purdy, a Friendship in Letters: Selected Correspondence*. Toronto: McClelland and Stewart, 1993.

Lennox, John, ed. *Selected Letters of Margaret Laurence and Adele Wiseman*. Toronto: University of Toronto Press, 1997.

Morley, Patricia A. *Margaret Laurence: The Long Journey Home*. Montreal: McGill-Queen's University Press, 1991.

Morley, Patricia, A. *Margaret Laurence*. Boston: Twayne Publishers, 1981.

New, William, ed. *Margaret Laurence*. Toronto: McGraw-Hill Ryerson, 1977.

Powers, Lyall. *Alien Heart: The Life and Work of Margaret Laurence*. Winnipeg: University of Manitoba Press, 2003.

Riegel, Christian, ed. *Challenging Territory: The Writing of Margaret Laurence*. Edmonton: University of Alberta Press, 1997.

Staines, David, ed. *Margaret Laurence: Critical Reflections*. Ottawa: University of Ottawa Press, 2001.

Thomas, Clara. *The Manawaka World of Margaret Laurence*. Toronto: McClelland and Stewart, 1975.

Wainwright, J.A., ed. *A Very Large Soul: Selected Letters from Margaret Laurence to Canadian Writers*. Dunvegan, ON: Cormorant Books, 1995.

Woodcock, George, ed. *A Place to Stand On: Essays by and about Margaret Laurence*. Edmonton: NeWest Press, 1983.

Xiques, Donez. *Margaret Laurence: The Making of a Writer*. Toronto: University of Toronto Press, in press.

Bonheur d'occasion, 1993, Montréal: Boréal, collection Boréal Compact, no. 50, translated as *The Tin Flute*, translated by Alan Brown, 1991, Toronto: McClelland and Stewart.

La Petite Poule d'eau, 1993, Montréal: Boréal, collection Boréal Compact, no. 48, translated as *Where Nests the Water Hen*, translated by Harry L. Binsse, 1989, Toronto: McClelland and Stewart.

Alexandre Chenevert, 1995, Montréal: Boréal, collection Boréal Compact, no. 62, translated as *The Cashier*, translated by Harry Binsse, 1990, Toronto: McClelland and Stewart.

Rue Deschambault, 1993, Montréal: Boréal, collection Boréal Compact, no. 46, translated as *Street of Riches*, translated by Harry Binsse, 1991, Toronto: McClelland and Stewart.

La Montagne secrète, 1994, Montréal: Boréal, collection Boréal Compact, no. 53, translated as *The Hidden Mountain*, translated by Harry Binsse, 1975, Toronto: McClelland and Stewart.

La Route d'Altamont, 1993, Montréal: Boréal, collection Boréal Compact, no. 47, translated as *The Road Past Altamont*, translated by Joyce Marshall, 1989, Toronto: McClelland and Stewart.

La Rivière sans repos, 1995, Montréal: Boréal, collection Boréal Compact, no. 63, translated as *Windflower*, translated by Joyce Marshall, 1970, Toronto: McClelland and Stewart.

Cet été qui chantait, 1993, Montréal: Boréal, collection Boréal Compact, no. 45, translated as *Enchanted Summer*, translated by Joyce Marshall, 1976, Toronto: McClelland and Stewart.

Un jardin au bout du monde, 1994, Montréal: Boréal, collection Boréal Compact, no. 54, translated as *Garden in the Wind*, translated by Alan Brown, 1989, Toronto: McClelland and Stewart.

Ma vache Bossie, conte pour enfants [illustrations by Louise Pomminville], 1976, Montréal: Leméac; translated as *My Cow Bossie*, translated by Alan Brown, 1988, Toronto: McClelland and Stewart.

Ces enfants de ma vie, 1993, Montréal: Boréal, collection Boréal Compact, no. 49, translated as *Children of My Heart*, translated by Alan Brown, 1979, Toronto: McClelland and Stewart.

Fragiles lumières de la terre, écrits divers 1942-1970, 1996, Montréal: Boréal, collection Boréal Compact, no. 77, translated as *The Fragile Lights of Earth*, translated by Alan Brown, 1982, Toronto: McClelland and Stewart.

Courte-Queue, conte pour enfants, 1979 [illustrations by François Olivier], Montréal: Stanké, translated as *Cliptail*, translated by Alan Brown, 1983, Toronto: McClelland and Stewart.

De quoi t'ennuies-tu, Éveline?, 1988, Montréal: Boréal, collection Boréal Compact, no. 8 [suivi de *Ély! Ély! Ély!*].

La détresse et l'enchantement, 1988, Montréal, Boréal, collection Boréal Compact, no. 7, translated as *Enchantment and Sorrow*, translated by Patricia Claxton, 1987, Toronto: Lester & Orpen Dennys.

L'Espagnole et la Pékinoise, conte pour enfants [illustrations de Jean-Yves Ahern], 1986, Montréal: Boréal, translated as *The Tortoiseshell and the Pekinese*, translated by Patricia Claxton, 1989, Toronto: Doubleday Canada.

Ma chère petite sœur, lettres à Bernadette 1943-1970 [édition préparée par François Ricard], 1988, Montréal: Boréal, translated as *Letters to Bernadette*, translated by Patricia Claxton, 1990, Toronto: Lester & Orpen Dennys.

Mon cher grand fou : lettres à Marcel Carbotte, 1947-1979, édition préparée par Sophie Marcotte, avec la collaboration de François Ricard et Jane Everett, 2001, Montréal, Boréal.

Le Temps qui m'a manqué, suite inédite de La détresse et l'enchantement, édition préparée par François Ricard, Dominique Fortier et Jane Everett, 1997, Montréal: Boréal.

Contes pour enfants [illustrated by Nicole Lafond], 1998, Montréal: Boréal.

Le pays de Bonheur d'occasion et autres récits autobiographiques épars et inédits, édition préparée par François Ricard, Sophie Marcotte et Jane Everett, 2000, Montréal: Boréal.

For works published until 1978, consult Paul Socken, *Gabrielle Roy: An Annotated Bibliography*, Toronto: ECW Press, 1979.

For works published between 1979 and 1984, consult Richard M. Chadbourne, "Essai bibliographique: cinq ans d'études sur Gabrielle Roy 1979-1984," *Etudes littéraires* 17, 3: 597-609.

For works published after 1984 (but including those dating back to 1978), consult Lori Saint-Martin, *Lectures contemporaines de Gabrielle Roy: bibliographie analytique des etudes critiques 1978-1997*. Montréal: Boréal, 1998.

Babby, Ellen Reisman. *The Play of Language and Spectacle: A Structural Reading of Selected Texts by Gabrielle Roy*. Toronto: ECW Press, 1985.

Coleman, Patrick. *The Limits of Sympathy: Gabrielle Roy's The Tin Flute*. Toronto: ECW Press, 1993.

Harvey, Carol J. *Le Cycle manitobain de Gabrielle Roy*. Saint-Boniface: Editions des Plaines, 1993.

Hughes, Terrance. *Gabrielle Roy et Margaret Laurence : Deux chemins, une recherche*. Saint-Boniface: Editions du Blé, 1983.

Morency, Jean. *Un roman du regard. La Montagne secrète de Gabrielle Roy*. Québec: Centre de recherche en littérature québécoise, coll. « Essais » no. 3, 1986.

Ricard, François. *Gabrielle Roy, une vie*. Montréal: Boréal, 1996.

Romney, Claude and Estelle Dansereau, eds. *Portes de communications. Etudes discursives et stylistiques de l'œuvre de Gabrielle Roy*. Sainte-Foy: Presses de l'Université Laval, 1995.

Socken, Paul. *Concordance de Bonheur d'occasion de Gabrielle Roy*. Waterloo: University of Waterloo Press, 1982.

Socken, Paul. *Myth and Morality in Alexandre Chenevert by Gabrielle Roy*. Frankfurt on Main: Peter Lang, 1987.